A CRYPTOZOOLOGIST'S
GUIDE TO CURIOUS CREATURES

GASHADOKURO

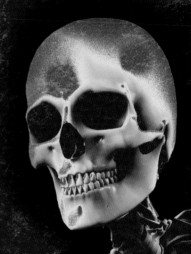

the Giant Skeleton

AND OTHER LEGENDARY CREATURES OF JAPAN

BY CRAIG BOUTLAND

Gareth Stevens
PUBLISHING

Please visit our website, www.garethstevens.com.
For a free color catalog of all our high-quality books,
call toll-free 1-800-542-2595 or fax 1-877-542-2596.

Cataloging-in-Publication Data

Names: Boutland, Craig.
Title: Gashadokuro the giant skeleton and other legendary creatures of Japan / Craig Boutland.
Description: New York : Gareth Stevens Publishing, 2019. | Series: A cryptozoologist's guide to curious creatures |
Includes glossary and index.
Identifiers: LCCN ISBN 9781538227152 (pbk.) | ISBN 9781538227145 (library bound) | ISBN 9781538227169
(6 pack)
Subjects: LCSH: Mythology, Japanese--Juvenile literature. | Animals, Mythical--Juvenile literature. |
Cryptozoology--Juvenile literature.
Classification: LCC BL2203.B68 2019 | DDC 398.2'0952--dc23

Published in 2019 by
Gareth Stevens Publishing
111 East 14th Street, Suite 349
New York, NY 10003

For Brown Bear Books Ltd:
Editor: Dawn Titmus
Designer: Lynne Lennon
Editorial Director: Lindsey Lowe
Children's Publisher: Anne O'Daly
Design Manager: Keith Davis
Picture Manager: Sophie Mortimer

Picture credits:
Front Cover: Public Domain
Interior: Getty Images: Wild Horizons, 29; **iStock:** cameranew, 15, EasyBuy3u, 14tr, fatido, 28, pius99, 17,
RichVintage, 5bc, 19; **Public Domain:** 1, As6673, 21b, Cryptid Wiki, 20, 21tr; **Robert Hunt Library:** 5tr, 7, 8,
9, 11, 13; **Shutterstock:** Aksara.k, 5bl, 14bl, beeboys, 26, Christopher Elwell, 10, Everett Historical, 23,
eye-blink, 27, Thanya Jones, 24, Amon Polin, 22, reptiles4all, 5br, 25; **Topfoto:** 16.

Brown Bear Books have made every attempt to contact the copyright holders.
If you have any information please contact licensing@brownbearbooks.co.uk

Manufactured in the United States of America
1 2 3 4 5 6 7 8 9 12 11 10

CPSIA compliance information: Batch #CS18GS. For further information contact Gareth Stevens, New York, New York at 1-800-542-2595.

CONTENTS

**WORDS IN THE GLOSSARY APPEAR IN BOLD TYPE
THE FIRST TIME THEY ARE USED IN THE TEXT.**

CURIOUS CREATURES

All over the world, there are stories about curious and amazing creatures. These animals often appear in **myths** and **legends**. In Puerto Rico, one story tells of a bloodsucking monster. In South Africa, there are **rumors** about a mysterious serpent that lives in a deep cave. In Russian **folklore**, there is a tale about a witch who traps children in her forest hut. Do these incredible creatures really exist? Or are they just stories?

Many people think such creatures do exist and say they have seen them. Some even claim they have photos and videos. The search for these creatures and other animals thought to be **extinct** is called cryptozoology. "Crypto" means "hidden," and zoology is the study of animals.

IN THIS BOOK

In Japan, there are many stories about legendary creatures. In this book, we look at the stories about giant skeletons called *gashadokuro*, mysterious water creatures known as *kappas*, a humanlike beast named the Hibagon, and a snake that spits venom called *tsuchinoko*. Now read on...

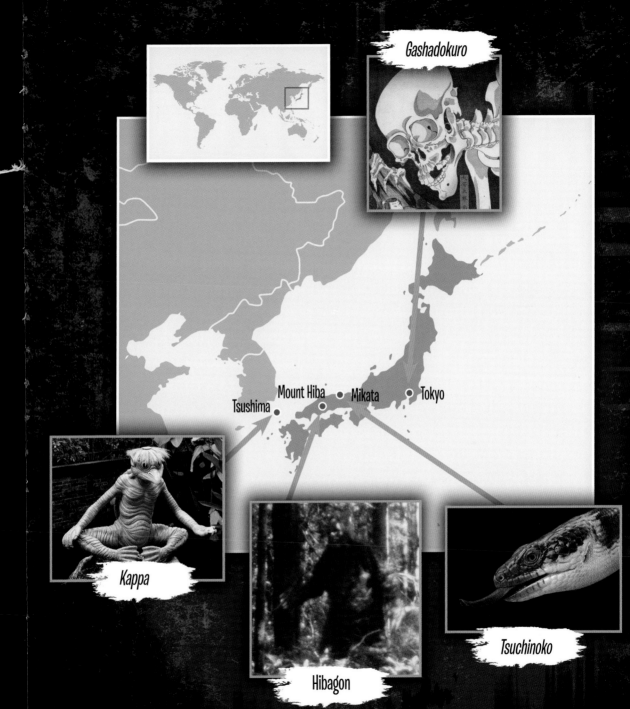

Gashadokuro

Tsushima • Mount Hiba • Mikata • Tokyo

Kappa

Hibagon

Tsuchinoko

THE GASHADOKURO

Japan has many **folktales** about **supernatural demons** and spirits. These beings are known as *yokai*, and the most terrifying of them all is the *gashadokuro* "starving skeleton." *Gashadokuro* are enormous beings made from the skeletons of people who have died in battle, or starved to death, but have not been buried. The skeletons roam around after midnight, looking for travelers. Then they bite off the heads of their victims and drink their blood while it is still warm. The only warning the victim gets is a ringing sound—*gashadokuro* are able to make themselves invisible and even to change shape when they want to, so they can sneak up on victims before they pounce.

Modern stories about the *gashadokuro* have been influenced by a **woodblock** print from about 1844. Japanese artist Utagawa Kuniyoshi made it, and it shows a giant skeleton about to attack a nobleman named Oya no Taro Mitsukuni. In many of the original stories, the *gashadokuro* were said to be made up of several skeletons, rather than being a single skeleton, and were 15 times bigger than a human being!

Part of the woodblock print by Utagawa Kuniyoshi, showing a giant skeleton attacking warring noblemen.

7

BORN ON THE BATTLEFIELDS

The original story of the *gashadokuro* tells how the creatures were created from the bones of warriors. They had died during a **rebellion** against the emperor, led by Taira no Masakado, who had declared himself the new emperor. During the **revolt**, Masakado had killed his own uncle. After his supporters were finally defeated, he was beheaded, and his head was buried in Edo (now Tokyo).

It was said that his daughter, Princess Takiyasha, decided to carry on fighting. She had been a nun in the past, but she was given a magic scroll that revealed the secrets of frog magic. Using **black magic**, she was able to create an army of demons. Another warrior, Oya no Taro Mitsukuni, arrived at Takiyasha's castle to find out about her rebellion.

The warrior Masakado was beheaded after the failure of his rebellion against the emperor.

In Kuniyoshi's print, Princess Takiyashi is seen reading from the magic scroll to summon her army.

She summoned a *gashadokuro*—a giant skeleton as tall as her castle—to fight Mitsukuni and his army.

Takiyashi's demon army used the souls of soldiers who had not been properly buried after they had died. They were reborn as ghosts and were angry about not having had a proper burial. The witchcraft of Takiyashi connected the anger of these dead soldiers, giving life to their skeletons. But despite her magic and the help of the *gashadokuro*, Takiyashi's rebellion was also defeated.

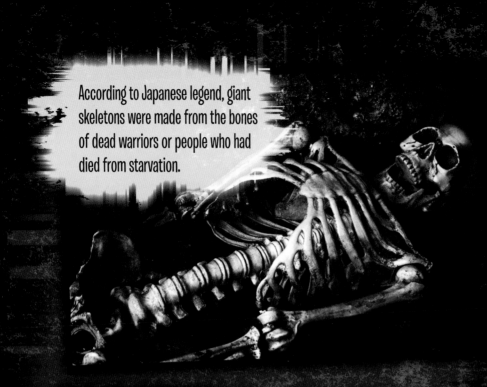

According to Japanese legend, giant skeletons were made from the bones of dead warriors or people who had died from starvation.

OTHER DEMONS

According to other versions of the legend, *gashadokuro* were created from the skeletons of people who had died from starvation as a result of **famine**. Collapsing and dying alone in their **barren** fields, with the rest of the community too weak to take care of the bodies properly, these ghostly victims were also able to unite their anger into huge skeletons. They took their revenge against living humans, killing them and drinking their blood in an attempt to come back to life.

In early Japanese history, famines happened regularly. Whole villages were sometimes wiped out when the annual harvest failed due to bad weather.

! FACT BEHIND THE LEGEND

Very little more is known about the *gashadokuro*. The story originated in times when conflict between warring Japanese clans was common. Perhaps it is a reflection of the fears and anxieties about death that constant warfare brings with it. In times of war, food is often scarce, and death can visit without warning.

Japanese noblemen and their families were often at war, fighting each other for control of a region.

THE
KAPPA

The *kappa* is one of Japan's most famous mythical creatures. It is a mysterious water-dwelling creature that lives in the lakes and rivers of the Japanese islands. In Japanese, "*kappa*" means "river child," and *kappa* are considered to be river demons, although the Japanese Shinto religion worships them as water gods. Whatever these creatures are, many people think they are more than just monsters from folklore, and cryptozoologists hope they might one day discover more about them.

Kappas are described as having blue-green skin like a **reptile** or **amphibian**, with rough scales and webbed feet. They are the size of a child of six to ten years old and walk upright on two legs. They have a beak and often have a shell on their back—some people describe them as being a cross between a monkey, a turtle, and a lizard. Their favorite foods are the flesh of children and cucumbers.

However, although *kappas* are said to lure people, particularly children, into the water so that they can drown and eat them, *kappas* are not thought to be all bad!

This illustration shows a group of *kappa* enjoying a **gruesome** meal in the form of a human arm.

Cucumbers are said to be one of the *kappas'* favorite foods–along with the flesh of children!

Far from being the enemies of the people, they have often been known to help humans—by helping farmers water their fields or supplying fresh fish for them to eat. They protect villages from flooding when the heavy rains come, and they also have healing powers, with particular skills in mending broken bones. Some stories describe how *kappas* help people who are injured or sick. In exchange for their help, people leave piles of cucumbers for them to eat.

GOOD MANNERS!

Kappas are extremely strong, despite their small size, and they are good swimmers. In the water, they will attack and kill humans, horses, and cows, and there is no escape. The *kappas'* strength comes from a flat area on top of its head. This is shaped like a saucer and must always be kept wet.

This statue of a mischievous-looking *kappa* decorates a pond in Japan.

14

☑ STRANGE BUT TRUE?

Some people think Japanese macaques, which are found throughout Japan, may be the source of the legend. Macaques are excellent swimmers, often sit in hot springs during the cold winters, and are known to wash their food in water. Other people think the now extinct Japanese otter could have been the original source of *kappa* sightings, while others say the stories are just exaggerated reports of Japanese giant salamanders, which are known to grab prey on riverbanks and drag it down into the water. Or perhaps the real explanation is that *kappas* were monks! In the 1500s, monks from Portugal arrived in Japan. They shaved circles in the hair on top of their heads and wore robes with hoods hanging down their backs—could these hoods have been mistaken for shells?

Japanese macaques bathe in hot springs and wash their food in water. Have people perhaps mistaken them for *kappas*?

Many *kappa* folktales describe how the creature loses its powers if its head dries out. But if a human comes across a *kappa* on land, one way to escape is to bow deeply in greeting. Kappas are very polite and will feel obliged to make a deep bow in return, tipping the water off its head. The creature is not able to get up from its bent position until the water is replaced!

! HOW STRANGE!

In June 2014, cryptozoologists were able to look at the **mummified remains** of what were claimed to be the foot, arm, and hand of a *kappa*. These went on display for the first time at the Miyakonojo Shimazu Residence on the island of Kyushu. The creature had supposedly been shot dead in 1818, but no one knew who had shot it, nor what had happened to the rest of the body. The Zuiryuji Temple in Osaka also claims to have *kappa* remains. The Osaka mummy has thin arms and teeth like needles, with strands of hair on its head. The Sosen-ji Temple in Tokyo keeps piles of cucumbers as offerings to the *kappa* and also claims to have a mummified *kappa* hand. However, none of these relics have ever been scientifically analyzed.

This is said to be a mummified *kappa*. Many sites in Japan claim to have the remains of a *kappa*.

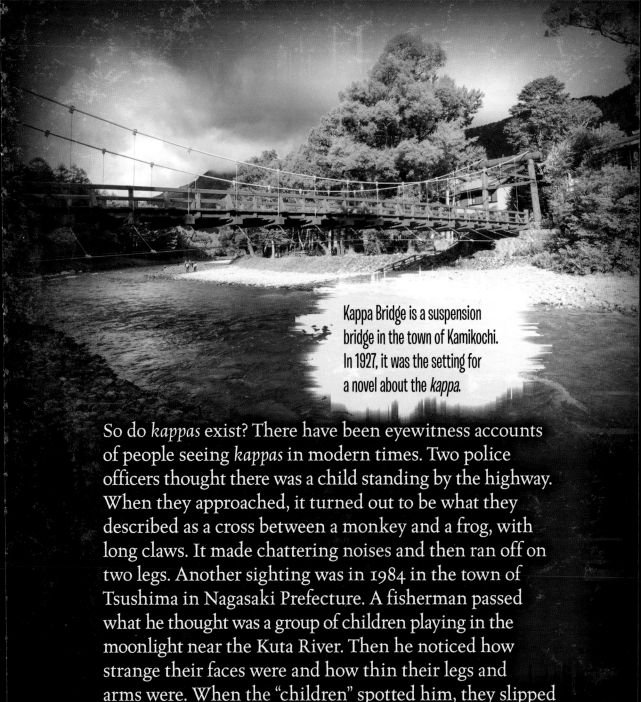

Kappa Bridge is a suspension bridge in the town of Kamikochi. In 1927, it was the setting for a novel about the *kappa*.

So do *kappas* exist? There have been eyewitness accounts of people seeing *kappas* in modern times. Two police officers thought there was a child standing by the highway. When they approached, it turned out to be what they described as a cross between a monkey and a frog, with long claws. It made chattering noises and then ran off on two legs. Another sighting was in 1984 in the town of Tsushima in Nagasaki Prefecture. A fisherman passed what he thought was a group of children playing in the moonlight near the Kuta River. Then he noticed how strange their faces were and how thin their legs and arms were. When the "children" spotted him, they slipped into the water. The next day, the fisherman found slimy footprints on the shore. Had he met a group of *kappas*?

THE HIBAGON

In the summer of 1970, a curious creature was seen lurking in the forests of the Mount Hiba national park, in Japan's northern Hiroshima Prefecture. One of the witnesses reported it was "about 5 feet [1.5 m] tall with a face like an **inverted** triangle, covered with **bristles**. [It had] a **snub nose**, and large, deep, glaring eyes." Another petrified witness said: "… the **stench** was what really got to me. He must have bathed in a **septic tank** and dried off with cow dung. I nearly passed out. Luckily … I managed to turn and run before it realized I was there."

Sightings of giant, humanlike beasts—such as Bigfoot in North America—have been reported for centuries in other parts of the world, but sightings of the Japanese "bigfoot" began only in 1970. The creature was named Hibagon (for Mount Hiba). Most eyewitnesses agreed on its height and said it had thick black or dark brown fur. Some eyewitnesses thought the hair was reddish, and some claimed it had a spot of white on its chest. Cryptozoologists believe the creature must have been some kind of bear, monkey, or ape, because it could switch from walking on all four limbs to walking upright, like a gorilla or chimpanzee.

Reports of a giant, humanlike beast emerged in Japan in 1970. Does a Japanese "Bigfoot" exist?

Although there has not been a sighting for many years, people still search for the Hibagon in the forests.

FLEETING ENCOUNTERS

The first sighting of the creature may have been by a group of elementary school students who were out picking wild mushrooms. Suddenly, they realized that a large, apelike creature was **lurching** noisily through the undergrowth.

In July 1970, a truck driver said he saw an apelike animal run across the road and disappear into the forest. Later that month, a farmer saw something running through his rice field near the town of Saijo in Hiroshima Prefecture. Twelve more sightings were soon reported, and in the winter, huge footprints were found in the snow.

There were other sightings of the Hibagon over the next four years. They were usually in the summer months and usually in forests alongside remote mountain roads.

Local people were afraid, and the police began to escort children to and from school. Then, on August 15, 1974, a driver spotted the Hibagon in trees beside the road and photographed it. Other eyewitnesses took more photographs, and even video footage, but all the images were too blurry to clearly identify the creature. Then, after the summer of 1974, reported sightings suddenly stopped.

Photos taken by eyewitnesses are blurry and indistinct.

The Hibagon is said to roam the forests around Mount Hiba.

FINAL APPEARANCES

In 1980, another humanlike beast was spotted running across a river near the town of Yamano. It was quickly nicknamed the "Yamagon." The beast was seen again in 1981 and finally in 1982. This last sighting was in Mitsugi, 18.5 miles (30 km) west of Yamano. The witness claimed the beast was 6 feet (2 m) tall and was carrying some kind of tool, like an axe.

Some cryptozoologists thought the Hibagon and Yamagon were probably giant apes or black bears that had escaped from captivity. The black bear would fit many of the descriptions, particularly the long triangular face and spot of white on the chest. Sometimes bears also walk on two legs. However, although black bears are native to Japan, they were believed to be extinct in the Hiroshima region. Whatever the creature was, there is no doubt that people were seeing something that was real. Just what it was, though, may never be known.

⚠ HOW STRANGE!

Some people had an alternative suggestion about the creature's identity. At the end of World War II (1939-1945), an American B-29 bomber dropped an atomic bomb on Hiroshima, killing 60,000 to 80,000 people. The bomb also had disastrous effects on the environment. Could the Hibagon be some kind of animal mutation caused by the blast, such as a macaque monkey that had then been chased out of its community and forced to live alone? The **speculation** continues to this day.

The atomic bomb dropped on the Japanese city of Hiroshima in August 1945 killed and injuried thousands and caused devastating damage.

23

THE TSUCHINOKO

Imagine a snake that spits venom, can roll along like a wheel, makes strange grunting noises, and, some say, can even speak! According to legend, this is a description of the mysterious *tsuchinoko* that lives in the remote mountains and forests of Shikoku, Honshu, and Kyushu Islands. Although people have told stories about the creature for hundreds of years, there have also been sightings that have led people to believe this **cryptid** might be more than just a folktale.

The *tsuchinoko* is said to live in remote mountains and forests, such as Iya Valley, pictured here, on Shikoku Island.

It's possible that the blue-tongued skink has been mistaken for curious snakelike creatures in Japan. This lizard originally comes from New Guinea, Australia, and Indonesia.

In many stories, the *tsuchinoko* has enormous eyes that are able to **hypnotize** people before it spits its poisonous venom. It moves in a straight line, rather than weaving from side to side, and can propel itself forward in leaps of up to 3 feet (1 m). It can also roll along like a wheel by grabbing its tail in its mouth.

According to legend, the *tsuchinoko* makes a wide variety of vocal sounds—including grunting, chirping, and high-pitched squeaking—and it has mastered human speech, telling people stories and playing tricks on them.

Many eyewitnesses have reported seeing a *tsuchinoko* in Mikata in Hyogo Prefecture.

It is possible that eyewitnesses have mistaken a common snake, such as a rat snake, for a *tsuchinoko*.

FACT OR FICTION?

Although many of the stories about *tsuchinoko* are clearly folktales, there have been numerous reports of actual sightings that began in the late 1900s and continue to this day. These eyewitness reports all give similar descriptions. The *tsuchinoko* is said to be between 2 to 3 feet (0.5 to 1 m) long, with large black or rusty red scales. It has a thin body, with a middle that bulges out to something like the width of a soda bottle, and it has a short, tapering tail. There is no doubt the eyewitnesses believe what they saw.

Some of the most frequently reported sightings have been in Mikata (now Kami) in Hyogo Prefecture on Honshu Island. In 2000, Mitsuko Arima claimed she saw a *tsuchinoko* swimming in a river. She said: "I can still see the eyes now. They were big and round and it looked like they were floating on the water. … I've lived for over 80 years but I've never seen anything like it in my life." Since then, there have been many more sightings.

Towns have organized hunts to try to find the *tsuchinoko*. They have offered big financial rewards to find this mysterious creature. In 2000, the town of Yoshii in Okayama Prefecture offered a reward of 20 million yen (about $200,000). In 2008, another major hunt in Itoigawa in Niigata Prefecture offered 100 million yen (about $880,300). No *tsuchinoko* specimens—dead or alive—have been accepted by scientists, and the rewards remain unclaimed!

Some people think the eyewitnesses have mistaken a common variety of snake for a *tsuchinoko*. They say any snake that has just eaten a large meal will have a swollen body. Some farmers who claimed to have found a *tsuchinoko* had actually found a grass snake or a rat snake. But Japan is a mountainous country with a population of about 127 million, and 93.5 percent live in cities along the coast. Much of the interior land is uncultivated. Perhaps a curious snakelike lizard, yet to be identified, lives in the remote mountains.

☑ FACT BEHIND THE LEGEND

Some *tsuchinoko* sightings in the 1970s described a creature with two front legs. Cryptozoologists think this is a description of yet another curious creature called the *notzuchitokage*. In 1974, two sightings described a red creature, with an upper body like a lizard, two legs, a head like a small crocodile, and a dark blue or black tongue. Researchers think this may actually be a blue-tongued skink. Although not native to Japan, it was a popular pet, and some may have escaped into the wild.

The two-legged worm lizard matches some descriptions of *tsuchinoko* and *notzuchitokage*, but worm lizards are usually found only in Mexico.

GLOSSARY

amphibian Cold-blooded animal with a backbone that can live in water and on land.

barren (of land) Having few or no plants.

black magic Magic that is associated with evil or bad actions.

bristle Short, stiff hair.

clan Large group of people who are related to each other.

cryptid Animal whose existence is not proven or is questioned.

demon Evil spirit or devil.

extinct No longer existing.

famine Extreme shortage of food.

folklore Beliefs and stories of a people handed down over generations.

folktale Traditional story.

gruesome Causing horror or disgust.

hypnotize Put a person or animal into a sleeplike state, but in which they can still hear sound and respond.

inverted Upside down.

legend Story from the past that many people believe to be true, but which cannot be checked.

lurching Moving awkwardly.

mummified remains Preserved dead body or parts of it.

myth Story often describing the early history of a people and their customs and beliefs, or to explain mysterious events; a person or thing that exists only in the imagination.

rebellion Opposition to a person or group in authority.

reptile Cold-blooded animal with a backbone that is covered with scaly skin and lays eggs.

revolt Fight violently against a ruler or government.

rumor Story that is circulating, but which has not been proved to be true.

septic tank Underground tank that holds human waste.

snub nose Short, wide nose.

speculation Ideas or guesses.

stench Very bad smell.

supernatural Unable to be explained by science.

woodblock Piece of wood with a design carved into it, used to make prints.

FURTHER INFORMATION

Books

Arnosky, Jim. **Monster Hunt: Exploring Mysterious Creatures.** New York, NY: Disney-Hyperion, 2011.

Gerhard, Ken. **A Menagerie of Mysterious Beasts: Encounters with Cryptid Creatures.** Woodbury, MN: Llewellyn Worldwide, 2016.

Halls, Kelly Milner, Rick Spears, and Roxyanne Young. **Tales of the Cryptids: Mysterious Creatures That May or May Not Exist.** Minneapolis, MN: Lerner Publishing Group, 2006.

Websites

wiki.kidzsearch.com/wiki/ Kappa_(folklore)
A page for kids about the kappa.

wiki.kidzsearch.com/wiki/ Cryptozoology
A page for kids about cryptozoology, with links to creatures.

www.newanimal.org/
A website on cryptozoology, with links to pages on creatures.

INDEX